ARNOLD SCHWARZENEGGER

ARNOLD SCHWARZENEGGER

A PORTRAIT
by GEORGE BUTLER

SIMON AND SCHUSTER
New York London Toronto Sydney Tokyo Singapore

Simon and Schuster
Simon & Schuster Building
Rockefeller Center
1230 Avenue of the Americas
New York, New York 10020

SIMON AND SCHUSTER and colophon are registered
trademarks of Simon & Schuster Inc.

Designed by Laurie Jewell
Printed and bound in West Germany by H. Stürtz AG in Würzburg.

1   3   5   7   9   10   8   6   4   2

Library of Congress Cataloging in Publication Data
Butler, George
Arnold Schwarzenegger: a portrait/by George Butler.
p.   cm.
1. Schwarzenegger, Arnold.   2. Bodybuilders—United States—
Biography.   3. Actors—United States—Biography.   I. Title.
[GV545.52.S38B88   1990]
646.7′5—dc20
[B]   90-9641
                                                                                CIP
ISBN 0-671-70146-0

This book is for
Franco Columbu and Charles Gaines,
who made this passage,
and Enrico Natali,
master craftsman of Ojai

all true friends

Canst thou draw out leviathan with an hook? or his tongue with a cord *which* thou lettest down?

2 Canst thou put an hook into his nose? or bore his jaw through with a thorn?

3 Will he make many supplications unto thee? will he speak soft *words* unto thee?

4 Will he make a covenant with thee? wilt thou take him for a servant for ever?

5 Wilt thou play with him as *with* a bird? or wilt thou bind him for thy maidens?

6 Shall the companions make a banquet of him? shall they part him among the merchants?

7 Canst thou fill his skin with barbed irons? or his head with fish spears?

8 Lay thine hand upon him, remember the battle, do no more.

9 Behold, the hope of him is in vain: shall not *one* be cast down even at the sight of him?

10 None *is so* fierce that dare stir him up: who then is able to stand before me?

11 Who hath prevented me, that I should repay *him? whatsoever is* under the whole heaven is mine.

12 I will not conceal his parts, nor his power, nor his comely proportion.

13 Who can discover the face of his garment? *or* who can come *to him* with his double bridle?

14 Who can open the doors of his face? his teeth *are* terrible round about.

15 *His* scales *are his* pride, shut up together *as with* a close seal.

16 One is so near to another, that no air can come between them.

17 They are joined one to another, they stick together, that they cannot be sundered.

18 By his neesings a light doth shine, and his eyes *are* like the eyelids of the morning.

19 Out of his mouth go burning lamps, *and* sparks of fire leap out.

20 Out of his nostrils goeth smoke, as *out* of a seething pot or caldron.

21 His breath kindleth coals, and a flame goeth out of his mouth.

22 In his neck remaineth strength, and sorrow is turned into joy before him.

23 The flakes of his flesh are joined together: they are firm in themselves; they cannot be moved.

24 His heart is as firm as a stone; yea, as hard as a piece of the nether *millstone.*

25 When he raiseth up himself, the mighty are afraid: by reason of breakings they purify themselves.

26 The sword of him that layeth at him cannot hold: the spear, the dart, nor the habergeon.

27 He esteemeth iron as straw, *and* brass as rotten wood.

28 The arrow cannot make him flee: slingstones are turned with him into stubble.

29 Darts are counted as stubble: he laugheth at the shaking of a spear.

30 Sharp stones *are* under him: he spreadeth sharp pointed things upon the mire.

31 He maketh the deep to boil like a pot: he maketh the sea like a pot of ointment.

32 He maketh a path to shine after him; *one* would think the deep *to be* hoary.

33 Upon earth there is not his like, who is made without fear.

34 He beholdeth all high *things:* he *is* a king over all the children of pride.

I was always dreaming about very powerful people. Dictators and things like that. I was always impressed by people who could be remembered for hundreds of years. Even like Jesus, being remembered for thousands of years.

A.S., 1975

Everybody wants to live forever . . . every man wants to be bigger than Dad . . .

Title song of *Pumping Iron,* 1976

ARNOLD SCHWARZENEGGER

He seems to float, suspending himself palms down on the rails of two back-to-back chairs. There are seven other men in the photograph but they fall away anonymously in his presence. His upper body—trapezius flexed, deltoids rolled forward, abdomen vacuumed into a small shadow—is an accumulation of striking details. The pectoral muscles beneath are large and sweeping. They glisten so shockingly in the air of the shabby room that the figure who bears them seems neither man nor woman to my awakening eye. Looking at this uncertain photograph today I can see strange contradictory images: his left arm lit and contoured as if it were the head of a carved ivory elephant; his own face tilting down to the right, eyes closed (a fragile death mask, with life, we know, to come), all the hubris (which we were to see too much of later) curiously absent.

I took this picture eighteen years ago, on September 16, 1972, in a backstage room at a bodybuilding contest in Brooklyn, New York, on the day I met Arnold Schwarzenegger. It was the earliest print I made of him in my darkroom and it was published shortly after in *The Village Voice*. Its publication, I suppose, signaled the coming of Muhammad—the vanguard of the national media—to the Mountain. The Mountain, Himself, with an ego that was slightly bigger than the Austrian Alps, was ready to receive them. Then and now.

A lot of what I did for the next ten years was to be the interpreter between Arnold and the press. This was essential (as well as unusual for a photographer/filmmaker), for without the highly successful publicity campaigns for the book *Pumping Iron* and the movie that followed, neither would have been funded or released. But these were, as well, rich and fulfilling years for me as an artist. And out of these years came an extraordinary friendship.

There was also a less obvious aspect to him that I hope my camera captures in this book. He had almost complete control over his body. It was an extraordinary thing to witness. For instance, when we gave the evening of bodybuilding at the Whitney Museum in 1976 (when Arnold appeared as the subject of the best attended—and perhaps most far out—event in the history of the museum), I asked him to trim down and appear as slender and unimposing as possible. He promptly lost thirty pounds of *muscle* in less than three weeks. On other occasions he simply reversed the procedure.

"How do you do this?" I asked.

"It's all in the mind," he replied. "You have to will the body to change."

I watched such changes. And then I watched him change in other ways. And change again. By the time we were through (our working relationship on the subject of bodybuilding ended in 1982–83), I had watched Arnold re-invent himself several times.

In the beginning he was an awkward bodybuilder in a dark subculture that America wanted no part of. At the end he was an international star ready to become the richest man in California and eventually the highest-paid movie actor in history.

This book is about his passage as a bodybuilder. It shows how he took his body and used it to achieve the American dream. It was my good luck to find him that night in Brooklyn and to travel with him as a friend and observer along the way.

Noticing where the best light falls, I place four leather boxes of pictures in mounted 11" × 14" mats on his massive oak desk. I open the first box and an impatient Arnold Schwarzenegger begins to look at the photographs in this book. I am confident he will be pleased. I have worked hard and meticulously in my darkroom, with the kind of professionalism Arnold always respects. Now he will see the result of ten years' effort: one hundred photographs of himself, many of which I have just printed for the first time.

As he looks at the images, in chronological order, beginning when I met him in 1972, his hands tremble. I am very surprised to notice this and I walk to the far side of his desk, hoping he will shake it off. But his hands continue to tremble. I sit on a chair and try to avoid looking at him. He has always been fascinated by my pictures and films. What is going through his mind?

It's a Friday afternoon. A month earlier I had called him from the East about these pictures. "You don't need to schedule a meeting," he said generously. "Phone me when you get here. I look at them right away."

I had arrived the previous Sunday at the Shangri-la Hotel in Santa Monica. I called. It took all week to get in to see him. And now, as his secretaries make clear, he is trying to leave for Palm Springs.

Within ten minutes, he has skimmed through all the photographs in a way that fails to disguise the intensity in his eyes. Then he leans back and utters a strange but revealing statement.

"George," he says, folding his hands and pressing them, knuckles toward me, on the edge of his desk, "I tell you something. Something I have learned. A man who gets rich finally becomes what he is. These pictures are from when I was becoming rich. Why don't you stop this sort of thing and make some money? And then we will know who you really are." He smiles—not unkindly—and gives me a mercurial gaze. I notice it is the same less-than-true look he had given many of these photographs as he sped through them.

"These photographs, you know . . ." He points at one of the last pictures in the collection. It shows him alone on the stage of the Sydney Opera House. "These photos are not me."

"Well, as we both know, a camera can't lie. That was you at the moment," I suggest, in what I hope is a helpful tone.

"But there's no pump. No monster arms. I look tiny."

"That picture's an exception. It's in between poses." I look at it —upside down on his desk. "It's a fine picture. You look ascendant."

"Come on." He guffaws. "I am not ascendant. Whatever that may mean . . ."

I try again. "It's still a wonderful story, these pictures. It catches you on the pivot of your life: the ten years that took you from being an unknown to becoming a superstar. And furthermore, these pictures and the movie *Pumping Iron* sort of . . . well—made it all possible."

Arnold's phone rings. He seizes it.

"Tell Maria I will be there very soon . . . very soon, I said." He hangs up and looks at me.

"I'd like to publish these pictures as a book," I say quietly, meeting his eyes. "And Cornell Capa has offered me an exhibition at the International Center of Photography in New York. I want to do these things with you the way we always have. I hope you'll collaborate. You can write an introduction. I'm willing to go to great lengths to please you. It's not just my story about you. It's your story. An unusual story about our time in America. It reminds me of what Alex Haley did when he wrote *The Autobiography of Malcolm X . . .*"

I should know better than to compare this work to the form and structure of that book, even though it is one I have always admired. It is not the most convincing example to pick in the age of Ronald Reagan and George Bush, especially in the company of their strongest supporter. Now I find myself facing down the brow of a confused and suspicious Austrian Oak. But I'm wrong. It is not Malcolm X that is bothering him the most. It is, of course, *The Bottom Line.*

"I plan my own autobiography, thank you. Swifty Lazar . . . you know?" He hesitates and peers at me.

I nod to show I know the agent in question. What Arnold did not know was that Lazar once rejected my proposal for a movie called *Pumping Iron* about an unknown Austrian with the name Schwarzenegger. But that was in another country (home of the Cannes Film Festival). At the time (1975) I was trying to finance the film against staggering resistance.

As I remember this, Arnold is inevitably moving the conversation onto his own turf: his own *new* turf, which he is beginning to control as well as anyone in Hollywood. I hear him energetically getting caught up in a deal. In this case, like a great mogul, he even supplies both sides of the conversation.

" 'I'll get you a million dollars in advance,' Swifty says.

"I say, 'No, I want five million!'

"Swifty says, 'That's the biggest book deal in history!' He says, 'Arnold, you are crazy.'

"I say, 'What do you expect, Swifty? You are the hustler!'

"Then Arnold" (he was now speaking *about* himself) "does another movie in three months. Ten weeks on the set. Bang! Twelve million plus 6 percent of the gross. Arnold establishes more value for Arnold! This allows Arnold to tell Swifty he has to pay ten million, making it twice as big as the biggest book deal in history. But already it is too late again, because now Arnold wants twenty million for his autobiography.

"Amazing!" Arnold says, shaking his head with the most complete satisfation.

"That's also a totally different book. Let this wet his chops," I reply. I was certain now and forever that all sense of traditionally lean, understated, parsimonious, New England values ended west of the Connecticut River on the border between my New Hampshire and that yuppie state, Vermont.

"No, George. It gets in the way. I am not ready yet. You remember"—and he pronounces these words very carefully—"THE MASTER PLAN."

We both laugh completely and easily. I haven't heard him mention "The Master Plan" in years. Somehow, I had assumed, with his vast success, that The Master Plan had been realized and discontinued. That Arnold's life was already in excess of any boy's dream . . .

I am—of course—wrong again. Guilty of making another assumption about Arnold. The Master Plan is still in place . . . purring as timelessly as the gold Rolex Oyster Perpetual on his wrist.

I start to remember the day in 1977 when we walked into Rolex on Fifth Avenue in New York and he charmed them into giving him the watch. As I think about that time, my friend blinks. He puts his big index fingers with the chewed-down fingernails to his eyelids and gently presses them. In the moment of his darkness, I can see him watching his life arc toward the twenty-first century.

I look carefully at his face as he solemnly rubs his eyes. Sitting across from me at his massive oak desk *is* the same man I met in 1972. But there have been some changes in the years between.

It just wasn't always quite like this . . .

Y ou have to look at yourself in the mirror and then visualize what you can be," Arnold often said when Charles Gaines and I first met him. But his vision of himself was not limited to the gym and bodybuilding. Even in the earliest days we spent with him in Venice, California, he was taking it beyond the Gold's Gym mirror.

He told us of a recurring dream. In it, he was king of all the earth and everyone looked up to him.

At that time, he was attending night school and living in a modest Santa Monica condominium with his girlfriend Barbara. So it didn't sound arrogant or even silly. Rather it was just *interesting* that a young man could go to sleep and dream such a dream as innocently as he reported it to us—over breakfast at the Pancake House on Ocean Boulevard.

What was more calculated was what he called "The Master Plan."

As I remember, it was a campy mix-up of Nietzschean philosophy and a Soviet Five-Year Plan. But before Gaines and I dismissed it as one more weird thing we had heard on a beach in California, we scratched our heads. Arnold, as we could see with our own eyes, was actually beginning to make it work. He was also the most disciplined and determined person either of us had ever met.

Arnold's Master Plan was more of a fifty-year plan than what, say, Lenin might have begun with (Arnold, could he have done so, would happily have planned for a millennium, if not eternity itself). Goals were established like the rungs of a ladder. They went up something like this:

"I will come to America, which is the country for me. Once here, I will become the greatest bodybuilder in history. While I am doing this I will learn perfect English and educate myself—but only with those things I need to

44th Street.
Manhattan, 1973.

know. I will get a college degree so I can get a business degree. Simultaneously I will make whatever money possible from bodybuilding and invest it in real estate where I will make the Big Money. I will go into the movies as an actor, producer and eventually director. By the time I am thirty, I will have starred in my first movie and I will be a millionaire.

"Since obvious wealth in California is the true source of power, I will collect houses, art and automobiles. I will see the world. Along the way I will learn to impress people and I will hone my mind to outwit all of them. I will shed exactly what I don't need at every step of the way: my old lives, small-time lawyers, agents, allies, and so forth.

"I will marry a glamorous and intelligent wife. By thirty-two I will have been invited to the White House . . ."

What made this plan difficult was the nature of the fellow in charge of it. Arnold was hard to imagine, much less deal with in the flesh. Most people were affronted by him; others laughed at him behind his back. As late as the mid-seventies it was impossible for anyone in the world to

Joe Weider confides in Arnold at a Mr. Olympia photo session in New York, as Ken Waller looks on.

One day, in July 1973, driving north on the San Diego Freeway for a meeting with bodybuilding czar Joe Weider, Charles Gaines turned to Arnold and said:

"Has it ever occurred to you that your body is like a classical piece of sculpture?"

From the backseat, looking into the driver's mirror, I could see Arnold's face lighting up like a birthday cake. He turned to Charles, then he turned to me, so smitten with this idea that he was actually speechless.

"What a brilliant idea," he finally said. "You know, in my ten years as a bodybuilder, I have never thought of that."

"You should look at an art history book, sometime," said Charles, lighting his own pipe.

"Immediately," replied Arnold. "Where can I find one?"

Thereafter, in every successive interview we arranged, Arnold worked on his rap about himself as a piece of sculpture. By the time we put on the live bodybuilding exhibition at the Whitney Museum in 1976 (as part of the promotion for the movie *Pumping Iron*), Arnold was ready to hold his own with the distinguished panel of art historians who lectured that night. New angles on his own career always appealed to him.

In the early seventies bodybuilding conducted itself in dark, dusty rooms. No matter how shabby the surroundings, the energy was just below the surface.

I wish I could experience the feeling President Kennedy had speaking to 50,000 people at one time and having them cheer and scream and be in agreement with whatever he said.

                                    A. S.

Wrist curls. Once I heard the great Connecticut bodybuilder Mike Katz say to Arnold as they were seated side by side on Roman chairs working their abdominals: "I hate these quiet boring exercises we have to do."

Arnold replied: "You may get bored, Mike. I use these exercises to think. I use every next minute to plan where I make my next dollar. That way, I am never bored!"

Flyes. Some bodybuilders say, "No pain, no gain." Arnold just said, "Pain is pleasure."

On the plane out of Los Angeles, after our first visit with Arnold, I asked Charles Gaines if he had Arnold's full mailing address. Arnold had given us a great time and I wanted to thank him.

"Yeah," Charles said, looking at me impishly.

"Well, do you need to look it up?" I asked, waiting for him to put down his cigar and pull out his notebook.

"Nope. Guess what the Oak's address is."

I tried to remember the street address of the gym.

"It's Box 1234, Santa Monica, California," said Charles, as if he had just ferreted the fox from his den. "This guy is really something. I mean what better personi-

Incline bench press. An expressive exercise.

ARNOLD SCHWARZENEGGER

fies him than that: Box 1234. He already has the sharpest address in the city and he's barely an arrived immigrant."

"You know what else?" I asked. "Did you see him open his mail? Well, he doesn't open his mail. The guy sits at his desk and looks at his letters against a bright light-bulb. That way he can see if there's any money in the envelope."

"This is his bodybuilding mail-order business?"

"Yeah. If it doesn't have money in it, he throws it in the wastebasket."

"I guess you better put a twenty-dollar bill in your thank-you letter," said Charles.

Gold's Gym was on Ocean Boulevard in Venice. In the early seventies, a lot of far-out people wandered its length. They were worldly characters and many of them thought they'd seen just about everything. A few even wandered into the gym. Arnold would spot them staring at him and ask Franco to hand him another five-thousand-pound plate . . .

Donkey-calf raises. I once saw a competitive bodybuilder standing in front of a mirror in the gym. He was concentrating as he flexed his muscles and, admiring what was in front of him, betrayed the very uncompetitive sin of self-love.

Arnold, on his way into the gym, paused to look at the younger man.

"You're fat," He said in a flat, objective voice.

"No way," said the bodybuilder indignantly. He reached under his arm and pinched at his obliques. "It's all muscle. I broke my water table last Tuesday. No fat and I'm not retaining water."

Arnold shrugged and ambled toward the changing room in his thong slippers. He started up the stairs.

"How can you tell where the fat is?" implored the younger man, following him.

Arnold paused at the balcony. Everyone in the gym was now watching. "Jump up and down."

The bodybuilder did as he was told.

"See, you're fat. Your waist is jiggling," Arnold said grinning.

"You mean . . ."

"Yes. It's simple," Arnold said. "If it jiggles, it's fat."

That was a pretty clear definition of America's preoccupation, I thought.

In April 1974, in association with a young filmmaker named Bill Benenson, I financed and produced a test film that was to be the pilot for the movie *Pumping Iron*. This was before the book was published.

Arnold came to Forest Park Amusement Center in Holyoke, Massachusetts, and gave a posing exhibition in front of three hundred people. In those days it was a big crowd.

I interviewed him and put together a selection of sixteen minutes of film. As raw footage of Arnold, this is worth a fortune today.

In June of that year, I invited about fifty friends, writers and potential investors to a screening at Townsend Studios in Manhattan. I believed I was really on top of something. It was exciting.

The lights dimmed and as soon as the screening began, my mouth went dry. The audience, most of whom had never seen or heard of Arnold, were laughing at him. When he revealed his torso and oiled himself, someone groaned loudly. What I thought was original and interesting appeared ugly and grotesque to everyone present.

At the end of the screening, after the crowd in Holyoke had given Arnold a standing ovation, the lights in New York came on. People I had known most of my life nervously fingered the photocopied handouts in their laps. Before I could begin the pitch I had rehearsed, a prize-winning writer stood up, getting everyone's attention.

"George. Don't go any further," he said in my direction. "We're all your friends and you must know the truth." He cleared his throat. "If you ever . . ." he said as sincerely as he could, "if you ever put this oaf Arnold Schwarzenegger on the screen, you and he will be laughed off Forty-second Street. Just put this film away and find something more interesting."

This had a moment to sink in. The group was perfectly silent.

"Am I being fair to George? Am I speaking for the room?" he asked.

There was a murmur of approval.

The audience filed out into the street making jokes about other things. My wife hugged me and said: "I don't think I've ever felt so sorry for anyone in my whole life."

Arnold and Joe Weider. In the background, on the left, is his brother Ben Weider, president of the International Federation of Bodybuilders. For his work on the international scene, Ben was recently considered for the Nobel Peace Prize.

Venice Beach. When he was in training for a contest (as he was here), he would train for three hours in the morning, have lunch and hit the beach—or at least the grassy area near the beach. Then he would sleep in the sun, efficiently tanning himself with subconscious adjustments to the angle of its beam.

He always woke up slowly and grumpily. When his energy returned —which it always did with a rush—he would become, once again, the center of attention. King of the beach.

ABOVE: *Franco upside-down.*
RIGHT: *(top) Woman
bodybuilder, 1973 (bottom)
Arnold.*

In a scene in Pumping Iron, *Arnold is asleep on the beach and then is
awoken to be reminded that he should be training for a contest. I
found a rising starlet to wake the Oak. She had been aggressively
tanning nearby and looked like she wanted to be filmed. As the
camera was placed on the tripod, she blanched.*

"Are you shooting this in 16-millimeter?" she asked.

"Yes," said the assistant cameraman.

*She stood up, looking piqued. "Well," she said, "I only do
35-millimeter." With that, she wandered away.*

*What she didn't understand was that we were using a blow-up
process that converts to 35-millimeter. Eddie Giuliani stood in as the
starlet and made it one of the funniest scenes in the movie.*

THE AUSTRIAN OAK

Birth: 30 July 1947

Mr. Europe

Mr. Universe—5 times

Mr. Olympia—7 times

Height: 6′2″

Competition Weight: c. 240 lbs

Normal Weight: c. 210 lbs

Chest 57″

Arms 22″

Waist 31″

Thighs 28″

Calves 20″

Serratus shot, for a woman looking in gym window. As some men might wink at a pretty girl looking their way, Arnold just flashed any one of dozens of muscles.

At traffic lights, his great elbow resting lazily on the car-window frame, Arnold would "shoot a tricep" at a nearby starlet without taking his hand off the wheel.

Arnold winning his fifth world professional championship. That afternoon while he was sitting quietly in the audience watching other contestants in the prejudging, a man muttering loudly tried to barge across a line of seats toward him.

A ruckus ensued and armed policemen escorted this stranger out to the streets. Watching this from the front of the auditorium I knew that Arnold, who lusted for fame and glory, must now pay its price.

I thought the man was crazy and dangerous. Arnold must have too. He looked very sober after this occurred.

Finally he slipped away. I found him later in his hotel quietly eating carrot cake.

In Cape Town I spent a morning at the beach photographing Arnold being photographed by Annie Leibovitz of Rolling Stone *magazine. She set up this photo with some young South Africans who were clearly fascinated by the specter of the once-again world champion.*

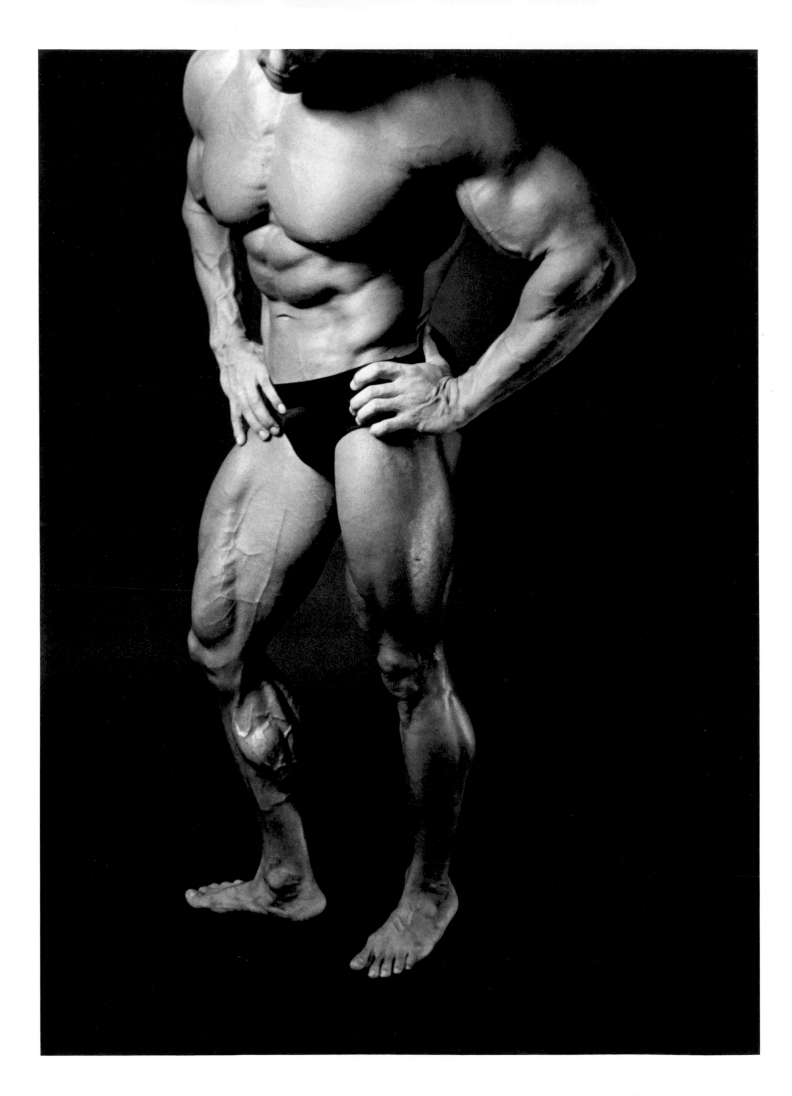

When Arnold began pumping iron as a teenager, his calves were the weakest part of his body—too low in his legs for his overall proportions—at least as he saw it.

So he trained (in a season, we once calculated, he would lift the equivalent of the *Q.E.2* off the ground), paying particular attention to his lower legs.

After ten years or so, these "bad" calves became so good they were finally called the best calves in the world —located directly beneath the best thighs, the best pecs, the best shoulders, and so forth. But how he fixed his calves remained a mystery to his rivals, and a rumor spread about a Mexican doctor who had successfully implanted some silicone there.

But if they had watched carefully when Arnold posed, they would have seen the calves flex . . . something silicone just won't do.

"You always have to stretch like the big cats," Arnold said. "I watch the big cats stretching in their cages when I go to the zoo."

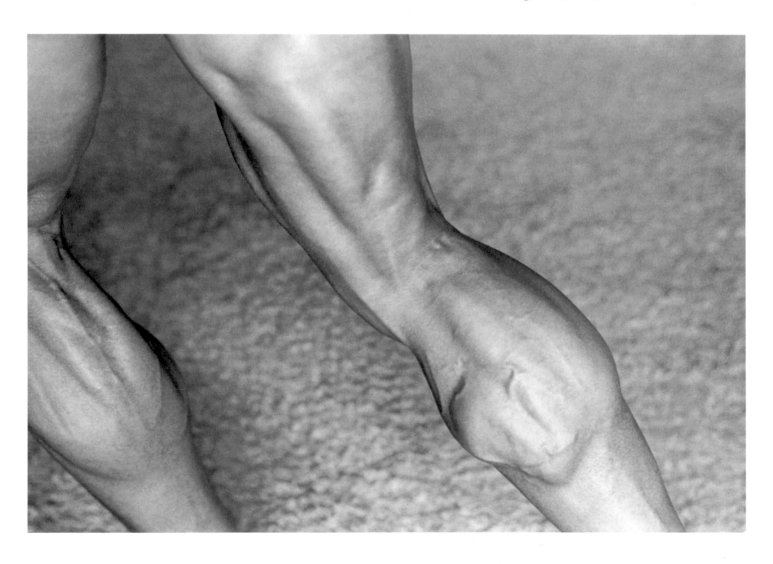

My definition of a sport is that it's a physical activity that involves competition. Since bodybuilders certainly train and then compete, we are certainly a sport.

The unique thing about bodybuilding is that when I compete, it is just me on a stage alone. There is no field, no bat, no ball, no skis, no skates. All other athletes have to use equipment, like a football. As soon as the football is thrown, where does the eye go? To the football. But I don't use anything in competition except myself.

It's just me up there. Me alone. No coach. No nothing.

A. S.

Before the Whitney Museum agreed to do our show, I also called the Museum of Modern Art to see if I could interest them in the art of bodybuilding. I was referred to a woman with an arch pitch in her voice.

I said as politely and gracefully as I could: "My name is George Butler. I'm interested in presenting a bodybuilding show at your museum."

Strangely, she sounded interested. "Yes, tell me about this," she said. "You're talking conceptual sculpture, I assume."

Now there was a phrase. "Well, I guess you could call it that," I said.

"Bodies on bodies," she said, imagining I don't know what. She went on. "It would be live in the sculpture gallery. One body on top of another in various abstractions. Have you shown here before? I recall your work. Was it from an article in *Art in America*?"

"Actually, no. I've published a book and I'm making a movie from it. Bodybuilding is . . ." She cut me off.

"Bodybuilding is end on end, is it not? I mean you talk geometric pyramids. Living Robert Morris sculpture. Lots of young men and women dancers."

"Actually, these are individuals who develop their own bodies."

"Bodybuilding one at a time..." she filled in for me.

"Men whose muscles increase in size when they pump up," I said.

Now there was silence.

"Did I hear you correctly? You're not the body sculptor who performs in Berlin?"

"No," I said. "I work here in the States. I'm from New Hampshire."

"I think there's a terrible mistake. You were not asked to call me?"

"No. I called myself," I said.

"You can't do that," she said. "Please get a proper recommendation from someone I know. I thought you were someone else."

She hung up. We went to the Whitney.

As much as possible when I filmed or photographed Arnold, I wanted to keep him in his true surroundings. Here I photographed his arm—with available light—against a piece of gym equipment.

While I was editing *Pumping Iron* and trying to raise the money to finish it, a number of prospective investors said words to this effect: "What you've screened of your movie is interesting, but will it draw people to the movie theaters?"

My answer was to demonstrate the public interest in bodybuilding by putting on an exhibition and inviting them to see the crowd for themselves.

I knew I couldn't get prospective investors to a regular bodybuilding show in Brooklyn, but perhaps a theater in New York was a possibility.

I looked into theaters in Manhattan. They were prohibitively expensive. The YMCA was booked. What was free? Well, perhaps a museum.

I knew instantly that I could get a crowd to see a bodybuilding show at a museum!

When the Whitney agreed to this bizarre event, I was asked by Palmer Wald, the curator in charge, how many people to expect. "About 300?" he asked.

That sounded right to me. I thought I could actually get 500. Standing room only. Impressive to investors.

On Wednesday, February 25, 1976, by 5:00 P.M. we had sold fewer than fifty tickets to "Articulate Muscle— The Body as Art." I thought I had a disaster on my hands.

What I had was a near disaster of another kind. By 7:30 that evening 3,000 people were standing elbow to elbow, neck to neck in the gallery on the fourth floor of the museum. Outside, it was snowing heavily and most of my investors (and hundreds of other people) were turned away at the door. Fortunately the doors were glass. My would-be investors saw members of the Whitney staff picking up money from the floor where it was thrown behind the cash register by the surging crowd who had ripped their tickets from the cashier's hand. This clearly gave them something to think about as they angrily departed.

It was the largest crowd for a single event in the history of the museum. Not only were they numerous, but they were also, many of them, impatient. All evening they interrupted the panel of distinguished art historians discussing the relationship of muscles to art by demanding that Arnold appear . . . immediately.

"All right. We're talking about a subject which is fascinating and quite present before our eyes, but which is rarely discussed in a public forum, that is to say, the representation of the muscular body in art. This evening we will also see the highly specialized type of body in action, that of the professional bodybuilder. Pumping Iron is subtitled The Art and Sport of Bodybuilding, which instantly raises the question for us of whether bodybuilding is indeed art. . . ."

Vicki Goldberg, *moderator, Whitney Museum symposium*

ARTICULATE MUSCLE
The Body as Art

A Live Exhibition
by
Arnold Schwarzenegger,
Frank Zane
& Ed Corney

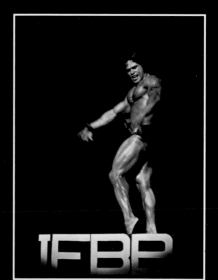
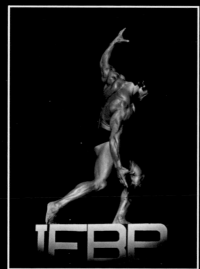
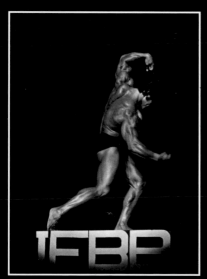

The Whitney Museum of American Art
Madison Avenue at 75th Street

Wednesday
February 25th 1976 at 8 PM

Photographs by George Butler from the forthcoming movie "PUMPING IRON"

Overall the evening was successful. Grace Glueck from *The New York Times* wrote an article. Candice Bergen and Arnold made *People* magazine. The bodybuilders got into the Whitney. Tom Armstrong, the director of the Whitney, even sent me a fine letter asking when I could dream up another event that would keep his museum on the cutting edge of the decade.

Finally (and most important), some investors, though miffed by the inaccessibility of it all, gave me enough money to keep editing for a month or two.

Souped-up bodies may propel us into a future new golden age with sins so original they aren't even a gleam in their father's eyes.

Colin Eisler
Professor of Fine Arts at the Institute of Fine Arts

Creation of Adam *by Michelangelo.* (The Bettmann Archive)

From a Medici tomb: Personification of Day *by Michelangelo.* (The Bettmann Archive)

Michelangelo's neo-Platonic concept of sculpture, bringing form out of the block, is somewhat analagous to the process of formal self-realization through bodybuilding that we have seen before us, in which exercise brings out a fresh manifestation of the divine original within.

Colin Eisler

I'm actually in heaven, being here tonight and having it happen the way it never happened before. People are ashamed of looking at the body and it's time to change that.

A.S.

Sometimes even a good friend can be a rascal. I'm sure I've taken advantage of my friendship with Arnold as he has with me.

One anecdote that doesn't wash in Arnold's repertory for his press interviews has to do with his very earliest days in America.

According to Arnold, he and Franco earned their living when they first arrived in Los Angeles with a bricklaying business (true). "We called our company Pumping Bricks," Arnold has been quoted as saying (untrue).

The fact of the matter is that Charles Gaines invented the term "Pumping Iron" in late 1974 as the title for our book. The term describes the sport beautifully. I don't believe Arnold when he claims to have used the phrase "Pumping Bricks" five or six years earlier.

But it's very flattering to the authors of the book Pumping Iron *that their world-famous subject would want to claim a prior ownership of its variable form.*

A few months after the Whitney Museum show, I was in a taxi with Rusty Unger and Candy Bergen. Candy was then reporting a monthly segment for the *Today* show. One of her segments was about Arnold. When it was shown, it was of course a big boost for my struggling movie.

"You know, George, Arnold and bodybuilding have peaked. It's all gone about as far as it can," Candy said as we waited at a stop light on Fifth Avenue.

I was a little taken aback by this statement.

"I disagree," I said evenly.

"Come on," said Rusty, who has one of the most beguiling voices I know. "You should listen to Candy."

"I promise it's here to stay." I paused, realizing that I was the straight man between the wits. But tunnel-visioned as I was I could not help myself. I went further. "It's the most efficient form of exercise. It's here to stay, and Arnold is going to be the governor of California one day."

That, of course, did it. There were hoots of laughter.

"And one day Ronald Reagan will be president," suggested Candy. "How can you say such things? It's a fad and it's about over." Candy opened her blue eyes and gave me a perfect, disarming look. Then she smiled sympathetically.

Now it was Rusty's turn. She was pursing her lips and thinking. "Oh, yes, I got it," she said triumphantly. "Now I remember. Listen to this. There was a contest at a famous New York restaurant—read Elaine's—to name this new movie about bodybuilding." She paused for effect. "The title that won was not *Pumping Iron*."

"Ooh, what was it?" Candy asked quickly.

"*For Whom the Bar Bells*," replied Rusty, not missing a beat.

The Rhine. Before going to the Cannes Film Festival with the movie in 1977, Arnold invited me to visit Austria and Germany. On this May afternoon we were traveling with friends from Vienna to Munich, where Arnold lived before coming to America. Germany is the second of his three countries.

85

Although the sun had set, it was still reflecting on the clouds over Vienna, illuminating the old city, making the blooming chestnut trees greener still. All day I had smelled their blossoms, right from the first steps of my morning run with Arnold in the park near our hotel.

In a city of parks, all the parks and even the sidewalks were filled with people strolling or sitting on benches while their children played. It was a perfect May evening in an old city where order had prevailed for centuries.

In rare, un-raucous accord with dignity, beauty and restraint, Arnold and a car full of bodybuilding cronies were slowly cruising down a long boulevard lined with oaks and maples. We drew up to a light on the corner of a park. As the car silently came to a stop, I noticed some elderly Viennese standing at the entry of a small Greek Revival concert hall. They were dressed in black tie and long pastel dresses, waiting for a concert to begin, fitting perfectly into their civilized surroundings, almost as if they had appeared from another century.

Theirs was the kind of evening I had quietly lobbied for since my arrival in Austria. But when I suggested to Arnold that it might be interesting to attend the opera, he said it was out of season.

"George, we go to concert in the winter when it's cold outside and we are not skiing. Then we hear Strauss."

"Well, Oak, how about a little Mozart in the park? There must be outdoor concerts this time of year," I said hopefully.

Arnold wanted to be a good host and he really was concerned about my interests. He looked into the matter. "Shirley MacLaine is dancing at the Opera House," he reported. "I hear she is fantastic, but even I cannot get tickets. She is sold out." I was not exactly unhappy to learn this.

But here, fifty feet away, was the kind of evening I coveted—after all this running around in expensive automobiles. I took out a pen and wrote down the name of the hall and the cross streets with the idea of coming back on another evening alone. Arnold noticed the concertgoers and when he did, he snapped to life. He spoke abruptly and

In Vienna we ate some incredible meals. Then we toured the cafés and ate Viennese pastry and strudel until I thought all of us would become sick.

"Isn't this excessive?" I asked Arnold.

"Of course," he replied. "We are fooling the body again."

"Yeah?"

"The body is very lazy. It gets into a routine. It does what it thinks it's supposed to do. So just when the body thinks that it can metabolize my high-protein, low-carbohydrate diet, I plunder it. Suddenly the body must work again. What is this sachertorte that has arrived for breakfast? Now the body must think instantly and be ready for the next ambush; for example, when I return to Santa Monica and Ken Waller brings a twenty-gallon drum of ice cream to my house at 2 A.M."

A few years later, Arnold was visiting the East and joined me for a morning run. He noticed I was doing the same stretching exercises I always do before loping off into the mist.

"Fool the body," he said. "Like this . . ."

He showed me a number of new stretching exercises.

"Do you ever run backwards," I asked, "just to fool the body?"

"Of course" he said.

the leather-jacketed Austrians beside me swung forward on the seat. Whatever he was saying brought them to a jittery attention as they craned around me looking out the window. The driver revved the engine and played the horn loudly. The well-dressed patrons turned our way, their faces wrinkling with displeasure at the disturbance. The stop light changed.

Arnold thrust his head out the window, put his hands to his lips and shouted, "————!" one of the crudest epithets in his language. The music lovers' mouths opened in horror, like the exaggerated faces of a Goya painting. As we departed in a tremendous roar of power and hot rubber, I turned around and saw an old man with medals on his evening clothes bouncing like a broken puppet, shaking his cane at us from the steps of the concert hall. His face was ready to explode.

This brought a triumphant roar of approval from Arnold and his friends. It was just the reaction they wanted to provoke.

Thirty minutes later, we reached a Bavarian restaurant in the woods on the side of a hill where Arnold had booked a table for dinner. Arnold knew I was ashamed of his behavior. The others sensed this and tried not to meet my eyes.

Arnold began focusing on my dismay. Schnapps was served. Arnold raised his glass.

"You should not be so . . ."

"Judgmental," I replied, sarcastically.

"Exactly," said Arnold. "But George, you have to understand what it was to grow up here. Those people who dress up and speak only to each other are the ones who make it very difficult for me and my friends to get ahead in Austria. They despise us and stop us every step of the way in education, in jobs, in life. That is why I go to America. You have opportunities. Many of us do not."

Looking genuinely in my eyes, he raised his glass. "To America," he said.

There was a pause as everyone looked at each other and then turned to Arnold, whose eyes glowed in the candlelight.

In unison, they said: "To America."

I am a Leo. If you believe this kind of thing, then you find out that Leos are more aggressive people than any other people and they are more physical than any others. I believe in this a little bit. Not everything, but a little bit. Because when I read what the lion is supposed to be and I check what I am, it's exactly the same thing. So that's why I believe in it.

A. S.

"Is there enough light?"

"Oh, it's wonderful," I said, covetously.

"No. Tomorrow it's better." He drove on, leaving the house behind. "Tomorrow we take a family portrait," he said, spreading his fingers above the steering wheel as he assembled this group in his head.

That night, at a dinner with his whole family of admiring, attractive cousins, Aurelia Schwarzenegger talked to me about her son with the help of an English-speaking relative.

"Many winter nights, after he had finished his preparation for school and thought his father was asleep, Arnold would hitchhike down the mountains to the soccer stadium in Graz. There, under the concrete stands, was the only collection of barbells in this part of Austria. He would lift them for hours. And then, after he had finished, this fourteen-year-old boy would come home. Sometimes there were no cars on the road to give him a ride and he would arrive in the early light to be picked up by a tank that took him to school. It was an American tank, because they were still occupying Austria and Arnold was very friendly with the soldiers."

Hearing the end of this story, Arnold leaned across the table. "And sometimes," he interrupted, opening his eyes widely in his boyish, expressive way, "I would be locked out and I would sleep in the barn with the animals. What do you call the place cows sleep?"

"A manger," I suggested portentously.

"That's it! I would sleep in the straw with the calves and oxen and forest horses. It was very warm and cozy. Waah!"

"Arnold!" shrieked an elderly relative beside him as he bearhugged her with both arms.

"As warm as this?" He flexed an exposed tricep for the table and flared it sensuously as he pretended to hug this woman to death. Everyone screamed and clapped in mock-catholic horror.

The next morning, I tried to persuade Arnold to do the picture at his childhood home. Instead he drove down the mountain to Graz. He wanted to show me the new house he had bought for his mother. He wanted the picture taken there, instead.

My upbringing contributed a lot to my success. My father was a police officer and wanted his family to be the perfect example to the town. We couldn't do anything bad. He was very strict, checking out everything . . . if we were clean, if our shoes were brushed. I was brought up under great discipline, which meant that when I made up my mind I had to follow through. I had a master plan from the moment I arrived in America. That's still in me. Every year I set a goal: to win the Mr. Olympia or to get so many units in business school, to make a certain amount of money, to travel to five or six different countries. Every year I make a plan. I do it. It will be done.

A. S.

As a child, Arnold determined, from seeing movies and reading comic books and muscle magazines, that he would become a bodybuilder. Reg Park, one of the great bodybuilders of the time, was his idol. In the beginning, as a young teenager, Arnold did not even have a set of weights at home. Here he shows me how he did isometric exercises with whatever equipment was available.

100

Arnold's childhood friends gave a dinner in a big beamed room that looked out on the mountains through open windows. We sat at wooden tables, about fifty strong, and watched as platters of steaming food arrived. The main course, nicely browned on the outside, reminded me of Alabama fried catfish.

But it was not fish when I cut into it. Arnold saw me examining it cautiously. He leaned across the table and spoke to me in English, a language no one in the room appeared to understand well.

"When I won my first world championship," Arnold said, "I came back here and the newspapers from Graz and Vienna asked me how I did it." He smiled broadly, revealing the large chink in his front teeth. "I replied, 'The secret source of my protein comes from eating bull's balls. Anyone can become a champion if they just eat enough of them.' "

Everyone at the table had stopped eating to try to determine what Arnold was saying to me. The Austrian Oak continued comfortably in English.

"Before the newspapers could print this story, I contacted the principal meat suppliers of the country and made arrangements to get a cut of their profits when the run on testicles began. Very soon, of course, every high-school athlete in Austria was demanding to eat these things. No one had ever eaten them before. They were cheap. The profit margin grew overnight. I made a small fortune! Ten years later I am still making money from local butchers. . . . So, George, you must help in perpetuating my business . . ." He made a motion for me to start eating.

When I hesitated Arnold turned to his friends and spoke to them in German. They exploded in laughter.

"My friends ask me why you are not a champion like me," he said, this time in English. "I tell them, only because you do not eat Arnold's Protein Burger!"

Arnold with his mother and Hildegarde Koroschetz. After I took this picture, Hildegarde, who is a cousin of Arnold's, came and drew a picture of a house with a smoking chimney in my notebook and signed her name beneath it. She was very shy around Arnold and just old enough to appreciate him as a famous man who had come home from America to visit her village of Thal. She asked me to give this to my son, Desmond, who was her age and was born four days after I met Arnold.

In the spring of 1977 Bobby Zarem introduced me to Suzanne St. Pierre, a producer from *60 Minutes*, the CBS news program. That day he wickedly took us to lunch at the Pierre Hotel in Manhattan.

Like all reporters, she was very skeptical in the beginning, certain that the movie was a fluke, that there was some sort of bizarre homosexual cabal or drug ring involved and at the very least that someone was making a fortune by exploiting bodybuilding.

Although I think I made a very good case that none of this was true, I found out in the next weeks that she was doing the rounds of all my contacts, trying hard to poke a hole in our fragile enterprise.

Finally, in late April, Arnold called from California.

"I think this woman from *60 Minutes* is very smart," he said.

"You're right," I replied. "So . . ."

"She asks very hard questions about you, George."

"That's OK. I think the best thing is to be open. Always tell a journalist everything. The worst thing that can happen is for her to discover something about the movie that we have not told her."

"I agree. But she is really pressing me. She wants to know what you and Charles get out of the book. They are very detailed, her questions."

"Well, they're coming to the Cannes Film Festival, so they must be committed to the piece. That's the most important thing. We can take care of the rest."

When they arrived at Cannes, this time with a British crew, the interrogation continued.

Finally it went too far.

"I almost lose respect for these journalists," Arnold said to me after dinner one night. "You know that soundman who was recording us today?"

"Yes."

"When he is putting on my radio mike he says in a very innocent voice: 'Tell me, what is George really like? He must be doing something wrong. You can tell me. I just come from England to be here.' And you know, George, I know that someone high up in New York has briefed him to ask very carefully arranged questions and try to pry information out of me about you."

After leaving Austria, we went to France where Pumping Iron *was opening at the Cannes Film Festival. The distributors got us involved with a zany French count. It was his inspiration to bring* all *the girls from Crazy Horse (the famous nightclub in Paris) down to the beach next to the Croisette.*

There, he outfitted them in long dresses and summer hats. Arnold would then, somehow, contrast his body with theirs. He did. Fifty thousand people, mostly with cameras, surrounded Arnold and his flowery backdrops.

"And they do the same thing to me about you, Arnold," I said.

He cleared his throat. "You know I never do it," he said. "I never let you down. We are a team. We have a job to do."

During these years Arnold was always like this. Always true. Never double in his dealings with me. He always had an ambitious agenda but he made my work of promoting and distributing our film a pleasure, because he always backed me up.

Over the years I have had my share of unpleasant dealings in the movie business, but with Arnold, it was always a fine experience to do things together.

Finally, in the autumn of 1977, Suzanne St. Pierre produced a piece called "Pumping Gold," reported by Morley Safer. It was a good piece of journalism and I had a small revenge for all the shots they tried to take at me. Typically, Arnold pointed out this triumph before I noticed it myself.

"George," he said, in another call from California, "these high-class, educated journalists miss the basic facts."

"Oh, yeah."

"You know how CBS is always so concerned about getting everything just right? Well, this time they really fucked up."

"Great. Tell me."

"You know how you are so vain about your magnificent legs?" he said, with a gleeful chuckle at my expense.

"Well . . ." I said, with great suspicion.

Arnold continued, "Remember the morning Suzanne filmed us running along the road in Antibes? The British cameraman sat in the trunk of the moving car and filmed you running, then he filmed me running? Well, on the broadcasts of the show on national television they only film me running alone . . ."

"Typical lack of interest in directors," I said.

"But they made a mistake in the editing room and they cut from my body to a close-up of your legs!"

"Wow."

"So now I have trained the most famous and the second most famous calves in the world," Arnold said proudly.

The true calf.

106   ARNOLD SCHWARZENEGGER

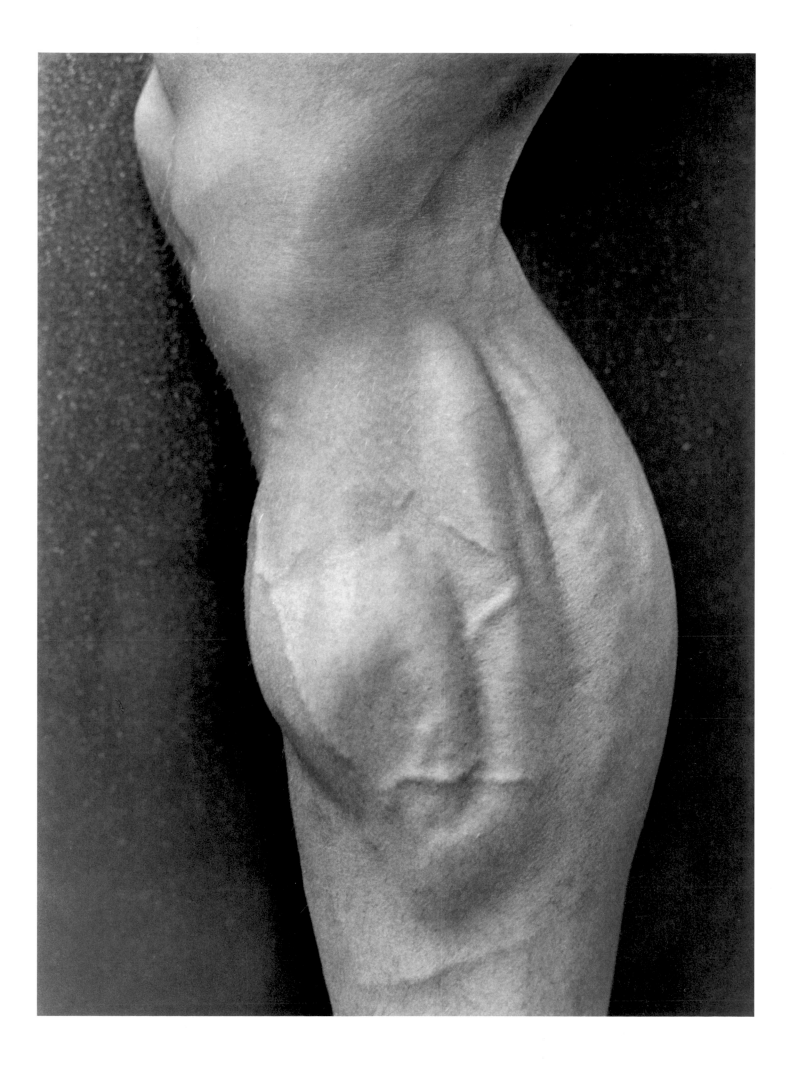

France. Frogmen with rubber knife.

"Well, I can assure you, Mr. Butler, with great authority, that they shall never be implemented at *our* Getty Museum in Malibu, California."

"I guess not," I said.

Without further pleasantry the lawyer rang off. I did not pursue the idea, wisely enough. Neither did Arnold, but I think he admired my enterprise—even if the results were disappointing.

Some months later I saw Norton Simon and we had a good laugh over the Getty's reaction to our plan. One day, we decided, they'd be old enough and lighthearted enough to take a bold step out.

What they missed would have been something they could never imagine. In my hands this was not going to be an embarrassing spectacle: I saw a gathering of several hundred people at dusk. Quite formal. Outside.

Not many people understand what a pump is. It must be experienced to be understood. It is the greatest feeling I get. I search for this pump because it means that my muscles will grow when I get it. I get a pump when the blood is running into my muscles. They become really tight with blood. Like the skin is going to explode any minute. It's like someone putting air in my muscles. It blows up. It feels fantastic.

A. S.

At a moment when the sun was about to slip down into the Pacific Ocean, just when its light was streaming east, I would signal to Arnold. He would mount a pedestal between the columns of that modern Roman villa up there on the hillside above the waves of the sea and throw a three quarter back pose.

As he became a modern Discobolus and the sun lit his skin and illuminated his muscles, the trustees, the directors, the curators, the guests and the lawyers of the museum would have been struck by his form and considerable presence. They would have enjoyed it and asked for more as Arnold completed his poses and bowed gracefully to their applause.

Of course, if Getty himself were still alive, he would have been in the front row, pleased as punch.

ARNOLD SCHWARZENEGGER

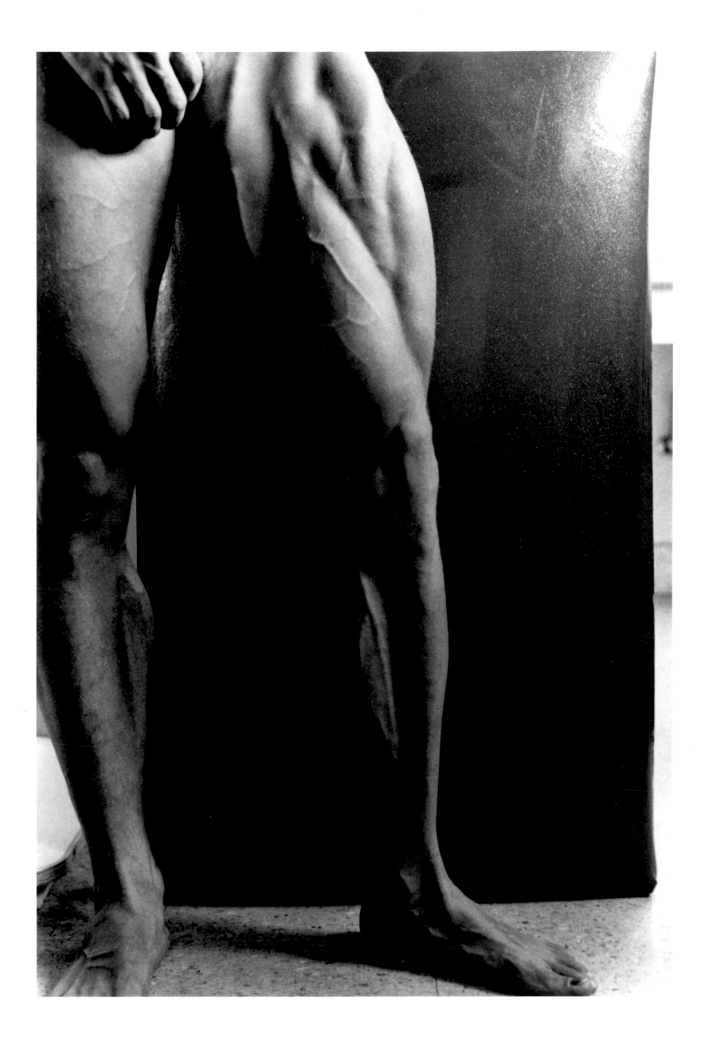

On a winter night, in the White Mountains of New Hampshire, about six months after Arnold's wedding, the phone rang. It was pretty late.

"Hello," I said, certain it was not a local call.

"Mr. Butler, my name is _____ and I'm doing an article on Arnold Schwarzenegger, for *The New York Times Magazine*. I wonder if I could ask you some questions?"

"Certainly . . . go ahead."

"Oh, no," she said. "The questions are fairly detailed. I must do the interview in person. Are you coming to New York at all . . . ?"

"In about three weeks."

"Good. I'll meet you. Wherever you like."

Three weeks later she met me in New York. "Do you mind if I record this?"

"Not at all," I replied.

For the next hour she went over Arnold's career with me, asking question after question, but always seeming a little flat. For a high-powered *New York Times* reporter she seemed strangely ignorant about her subject. She had not, as I began to realize, talked to many other people about Arnold. In fact, she didn't seem to know very much about him at all.

Eventually I asked, "Are you really doing a piece on Arnold?"

"Oh, yes," she replied, and asked a barrage of inconsequential questions. I went to the bookshelf, took down a copy of *Pumping Iron* and handed it to her. "In here," I said, "are the answers to these questions." Then as she skimmed through it I made tea.

She drew herself up slightly after I poured her tea.

"What about Arnold's Nazi collection?" she asked abruptly.

I looked at her in shock, not believing I'd heard right. "I don't understand."

"The Nazi collection," she said. "You have ears."

"I don't know what you're talking about."

"I mean his collection of Nazi memorabilia."

"Well, I've never seen it. Have you?"

She paused and picked up her tape recorder. "You can tell me off the record, George."

One day I heard a knock on my door. It was a young man looking like a muscular Huckleberry Finn. He was holding a copy of Pumping Iron.

"Good afternoon," he said. "I'm Bill Bixby, and I hear Arnold sometimes stays on this farm."

I nodded.

"Well, do you need some help haying? I like heavy bales, and I'm good at taking care of animals."

Bill got himself a job. But since he hitchhiked over from Wentworth, New Hampshire every morning, he left his copy of Pumping Iron *with me. He thought Arnold might possibly drop in some evening on his way to New York or Europe. He wanted to make sure the Oak signed it under any circumstance.*

A few weeks later I told Bill that Arnold and Maria were coming for the weekend. At 7 A.M. that Saturday morning, Arnold and I were sleepily lacing our running shoes on the front porch when we heard loud cheering and clapping from the direction of the barn. Most uncommon, I thought.

We stood up and saw Bill with all the top bodybuilders in the state waiting to meet their hero. A line of cars stretched down the road and disappeared into the maple trees.

"Have you still got my book?" Bill hollered happily.

1975 *Arnold at home in California with Barbara Outland, Jeff Bridges and Robert Fiore.*

I felt a pulse of anger. "I can't tell you anything other than it doesn't exist. Now you," I looked at her evenly, "tell me who told you this."

"I have a friend," she replied. "An individual who knows Arnold and informs me he keeps a collection of Nazi stuff—swords, uniforms, things like that. Keeps them in his bedroom."

This time I laughed at her. She was so dead serious and determined to uncover some slime on my friend. "Come on. Relax. I've photographed and filmed in every apartment and house Arnold has lived in since I met him. I've been in every room in these places. If he had such a collection, he's done a good job of making it vanish whenever I come to visit."

"Someone who worked with you on *Pumping Iron* corroborated this story."

"Oh, really, who was that?"

"He wants to remain anonymous."

"At least it wasn't a woman."

She smiled tightly.

"Look, _____, these are serious allegations. I think as a journalist if you choose to make innuendos with a fellow journalist you should reveal your sources and support them. Who are these phantom informers of yours?"

"I can't tell you," she said icily.

"If they amount to a hill of beans, you could."

She shrugged.

I thought of asking her to leave, but then I thought it was wiser to dismiss the story as completely as possible.

"In addition to the fact that I probably know as much about Arnold as anyone," I said, "bodybuilding is filled with gossip."

She at last gave me a nervous grin.

"Ever since I've been around Arnold," I continued, "I've heard all the stories about him. Bodybuilding is a small, tight circle. I've heard for ten years he's dying of cancer from taking steroids. More persistently I'm told wherever I travel in America that he lives on a kidney dialysis machine. I first heard that ten years ago. But ru-

1973 Arnold at my farm in New Hampshire with Delfina Rattazzi, Charles Gaines and David Thorne.

mors do not necessarily become facts. The facts are that he's as healthy as a horse. Why have I never heard even a suggestion about his alleged Nazi collection until today?"

She shrugged warily. "Maybe you just don't know."

"If Arnold's got a Nazi collection, I've never seen it or heard about it. Nor has anyone I know. That's pretty much all of Arnold's close friends, including Maria, the Kennedys, the Shrivers . . . is that enough?"

She sipped her tea busily.

I stood up. "Have you heard about Arnold's Bible collection?" I asked.

Her teacup and saucer rattled.

"Um . . . what?"

"Besides his trophies, which Arnold usually keeps in the garage, the only collection I've noticed are his Bibles."

"Bibles?"

"Bibles. The ones, by the way, without swastikas on the covers. Antiquarian Catholic Bibles. Mostly in German. He's always had them. In fact, the first time Charles Gaines and I went to dinner at his apartment in 1973 I remember him showing them to us. He was incredibly proud of them. He still has them in his living room and study."

She looked at me blankly.

"I wouldn't be surprised if he bought a Gutenberg one of these days. I expect that would interest him more than some old uniform. Maybe he'd give it to the Getty Museum. It's right next to where he lives."

She got up to leave.

"None of those uniforms would fit him anyway," I said.

After she left I had no more calls about Arnold's Nazi collection. But just to make sure, I asked Arnold himself.

"Arnold," I said the next time I saw him, "is there any basis whatsoever for this rumor?"

"No, George."

"There's nothing that I should know about on your behalf that I don't?"

"No, George, I said 'no,' " he replied, looking me in the eye.

Grannies on a park bench.

If most people in America felt trapped by their circumstances, Arnold did not. At every step he wanted to take advantage of every opportunity.

Once, before I met him, he broke a leg at a contest in South Africa. It happened because of a faulty platform that collapsed underneath him.

Instead of losing time suing the contest's promoter and falling into gloom over the lost training days, Arnold turned this event to his advantage. He studied his college courses in the hospital, filled the bodybuilding magazines with photos of himself being admired by pretty nurses (and more important, stories of his determination to come back stronger than ever). He ran his bodybuilding mail-order business by telephone into new heights of profit and used

whatever free time was left in the day to *think* of new ways to make money.

Enter Arnold.

The photos from this period are telling: they all show him with a glowing smile—even on his crutches when he was obviously in pain.

This positive attitude never ceased. Every moment of Arnold's life counted. He milked every person we met on our travels for information. Even when he was exhausted from promoting *Pumping Iron* in one city or another he would talk to the nearest passengers on the plane. Especially the businessmen.

I never saw him read a book for pleasure, or take a vacation that did not involve a business or promotional connection.

Mentzer, who was sitting on a bench next to the wall, jumped up as if to punch Arnold.

There was a tussle as other bodybuilders intervened to keep them apart. Ben Weider, his neck swelling in the collar of his white shirt and blue blazer, rushed into the center of the fray and disappeared from my view like a lone Napoleon disappearing into the steppes of Russia.

What had happened was this. Arnold had flown to Sydney as a CBS News commentator for the contest. When asked about the training everyone knew he was doing, he alluded to a sword-and-sorcery movie that was coming up. He wanted to get in shape for the Big Screen, he said.

At the beginning of this backstage competitors'

Embracing his old friend Joe Gold. A man of striking presence and character, Joe paid Arnold the compliment of coming to Australia to lend his support.

meeting, Oscar State, the British Olympic official who was supervising the proceedings (as he normally did), said to the competitors:

"Welcome to the 1980 Mr. Olympia contest. When I call your name come up and get your contestant's number."

Since Arnold had made no public announcement of his intention to compete, it was something of a surprise (but only to the most wishful of those present) when Oscar called out Arnold's name and the Oak stepped forward . . .

Mike Mentzer was so exasperated by this he said about the best thing anyone could possibly say when dealing with Arnold in a situation like this.

"He can't compete if we don't know he's competing."

"Why not?" said Arnold. "I'm going to win even if I don't compete. You might as well lose so you can say you competed against me."

Finally, Ben Weider, a master of international diplomacy (who, it must be remembered, was to be nominated within five years for a Nobel Peace Prize), sorted out the dispute. He convinced everyone that the contest would be fair and that since everyone else had spent a year in training it would be a shame for anyone not to compete . . .

The truth, as many of us in the room knew, was that Arnold had now positioned himself. As long as he was in respectable shape he would win.

I can hide my feelings under my muscles. Definitely. I can hide them as long as necessary. And when I feel they can come out, I let them out. I think this is fantastic. It's great to have control over my mind. Other people get mixed up. They can't control themselves. They can't go to work for a week or they can't talk on the phone because they're crying.

I can switch myself back and forth. When I'm training for a competition, I can be what some people call inhuman, but really I think it's more like being superhuman. Then after the competition, I can switch off and again be human and very emotional and so on.

A.S.

Backstage, check posing. The enormous strain of the forced comeback shows on Arnold's face. The charming, boyish Austrian I met in 1972, who did everything with such ingenuous curiosity and joy, my friend, had given way to a more severe, calculating champion.

In the middle of the competition, Franco Columbu (who was acting as Arnold's manager) noticed that the lighting in the opera house was uneven. The best light was on the left, whereas Arnold was on the darker, right side. In a contest, good lighting can be crucial.

Franco began yelling to Arnold to move. But in the pandemonium, Arnold could not hear.

So Franco leapt onstage. He spoke quickly to Arnold in German, drawing the attention of the other competitors. As they started to protest, Arnold stepped off the posing platform, seized Franco's arm and raised it in the air as if to introduce the champion to the crowd.

They gave Franco a standing ovation. While this cheering continued, Arnold elbowed his way back into the lineup on the left side of the platform and resumed posing in the best-lit position of all.

This interruption rattled the other competitors. What were Arnold and Franco discussing in German? I could see the confusion on their faces as they looked angrily toward Arnold. As they did so, the contest began swinging in Arnold's favor: the other competitors had just lost their concentration. Some had even lost their pump.

Meanwhile Franco leapt offstage into the front row where he continued yelling until Arnold was declared the winner.

146

Another psychological advantage Arnold had over his rivals was the swiftness with which he got in shape for the contest. By the time he arrived in Sydney and began acting like a champion ready to compete, he actually looked like a champion. How could anyone get in shape so quickly? It was almost a superhuman accomplishment. And who wanted to compete with a superhuman?

A lot of things come through my mind while I am posing. When I pose, a very good pose . . . let's say the most muscular pose. The audience starts screaming. In my mind I say to them, kind of like "Well, here it is . . . here is the best body . . . look at it and just freak out . . . because you're only going to see one of them. That's it." I let them know that what they get is mind-blowing. They are not going to get it tomorrow, not the next day. Maybe never again.

It's a once-in-a-lifetime experience. Especially since my career as a bodybuilder is almost over. I just hope they appreciate my body.

Obviously they do. I hear the applause.

A.S.

ARNOLD SCHWARZENEGGER

As the 1980s continued I found it increasingly difficult to work with Arnold. We stayed in touch. I had dinner with him often in New York and Los Angeles. Arnold and Maria came and stayed with me in New Hampshire. We talked a lot on the telephone, giving each other advice about things we each wanted to do. But our professional relationship was clearly changing and he was becoming distant and self-absorbed.

I understood this, and I also understood that he wanted to be a self-invented man and have absolute control over his own life. I was in the way of that. Besides, it was time for me to move on and I too was absorbed in my own projects.

So we drifted apart. What never changed and what I hope never will is the look of recognition he always gives me when we get together. It's got a very clean openness to it. And it's got history. It's really a brotherly look and I believe it will always endure between us. I'm sure he feels the same way about Charles Gaines and I'm sure the brotherhood is there, too.

There was a moment, however, a particular moment I knew my work with Arnold was really over. It occurred on the night before his wedding at a dinner he and his mother were giving for the Shrivers at the elegant Hyannisport Club.

I arrived in Massachusetts that afternoon, dressed for dinner at the hotel, put my Leica over my shoulder and a roll of film in my pocket. It's a small, unobtrusive black camera and I never use a flash. I joined Franco Columbu, who is always glad to see an old friend, and we walked into the dinner together. I had no particular plan to use my camera. In fact, I had hardly taken a picture of Arnold in five years.

As I arrived at the bar, one of Arnold's secretaries, whom I had known for years, moved purposefully across the room toward me. She had her mouth set in a tight smile.

"No cameras," she said.

I looked at her, taken aback. "But," I said, "I have no assignment and no plans to sell pictures. I always clear things with Arnold."

Arnold is an example of the precise man. When he worked in the gym, every single exercise was performed with a mathematical grace. Every motion counted: the grasp on the bar, the lift, the inhale at the moment of force, the exhale at the peak of the lift, the arc of the weight above the body (or sometimes below). Most bodybuilders get tired and sloppy. Not Arnold. He would actually pause before each set as his mind projected the motions he would require. I never saw him cheat a motion.

He never left the gym early.

At the time we worked together, I observed this iron discipline in all aspects of his personal life. If he bought a car, had a new telephone installed or fixed the roof of his condominium, he did each chore with the same sense of efficiency.

Being around him was instructive to me. Arnold's drive for perfection taught me a lot about my own life and I changed it accordingly. The way in which I approach the details of my life, my system of getting things done, has been influenced by what I learned from observing Arnold.

TITLES WON

1965 Jr. Mr. Europe (Germany)

1966 Best Built Man of Europe (Germany)

1966 Mr. Europe (Germany)

1966 International Powerlifting Championship (Germany)

1967 NABBA Mr. Universe, amateur (Great Britain)

1968 NABBA Mr. Universe, professional (Great Britain)

1968 German Powerlifting Championship

1968 IFBB Mr. International (Mexico)

1969 IFBB Mr. Universe, amateur (U.S.A.)

1969 NABBA Mr. Universe, professional (Great Britain)

1970 NABBA Mr. Universe, professional (Great Britain)

1970 Mr. World (U.S.A.)

1970 IFBB Mr. Olympia (U.S.A.)

1971 IFBB Mr. Olympia (France)

1972 IFBB Mr. Olympia (Germany)

1973 IFBB Mr. Olympia (U.S.A.)

1974 IFBB Mr. Olympia (U.S.A.)

1975 IFBB Mr. Olympia (South Africa)

1980 IFBB Mr. Olympia (Australia)

"I've been asked to impound all cameras," she said nervously.

I looked at a camera with a flash on the table where Franco Columbu was sitting. Other people had cameras.

"Well, if you ask me not to take pictures, I certainly won't," I said politely.

"Give me your camera. I'm very sorry," she said.

It was a moment almost like an impending car accident. I could see my whole experience with Arnold opening and closing like the pages of this book. I paused for that moment and I'm sure my face must have registered its profound shock. There was pain in her eyes, too.

Without further hesitation I gave her my camera. She smiled warmly as I put its cold, precise metal in her shaking hands.

"Take care of it. I've had it so long," I said.

"I know." She smiled. "I remember when I just came to work for Arnold wondering how that little camera could take so many pictures."

As she walked off with my Leica I clasped the single roll of film in my pocket instead of feeling the upset indignation I knew I should feel. Instead of screaming, "That's the fucking German camera that made Arnold famous!" I felt a wave of satisfaction. That this really was the end of the saga. It was as good a place as any, amidst the celebrities and the champagne, to call it a day.

Now I could relax at Arnold and Maria's wedding and celebrate with them. Someone else could take the pictures. They would tell the story of the arrived man and perhaps be edited for some future book on Arnold that would bring the new decades up to date.

The next day, on the way to the wedding, I rode with Charles and Patricia Gaines. We all liked the Shrivers and talked of their gracious hospitality.

As we came in sight of the church we saw limousines stacked up and spectators ten deep on the sidewalk behind a gallery of dozens of photographers and television crews.

I knew Charles and Patricia would look at me and smile.

They did.

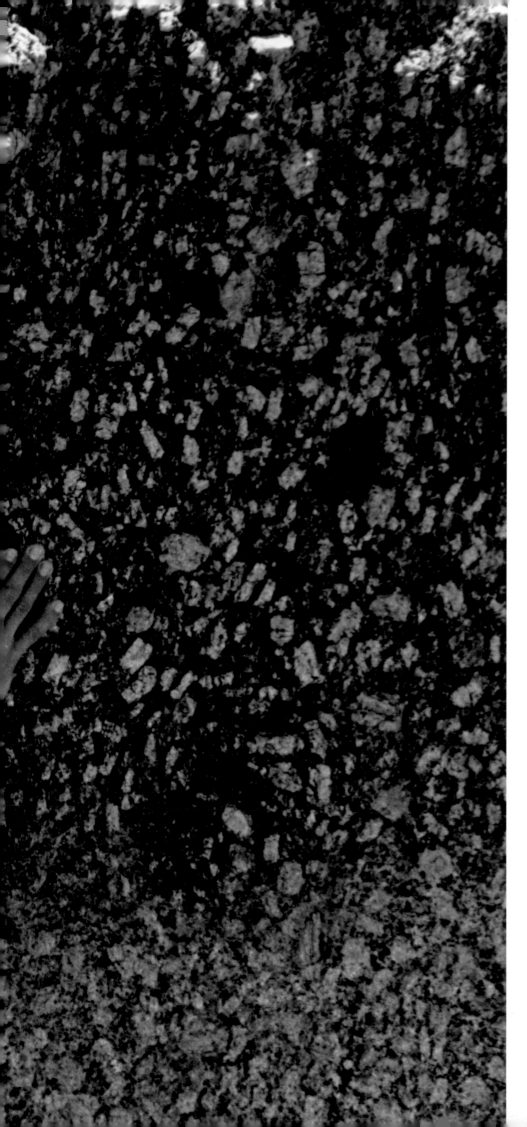

There's a book called Zen and the Art of Archery, *which was given to me by Enrico Natali. Enrico is the photographer who taught me most of what I know about the craft I practice.*

As I was admiring his present, he reminded me: "George, if you can learn to get yourself out of your pictures, they'll be good ones. This book will tell you a similar thing about archery: 'Shut your eyes as you aim for the bull's-eye.' "

This particular photograph may be the best picture I've taken of Arnold. It is certainly one of the most widely sought after.

I took it with one hand as I was following Arnold down through some boulders to the beach below. As he leaned against a big boulder to support himself, his back muscles caught the sunlight in a moment in which he was actually using them. By luck I snapped my shutter at that instant.

155

Charles Gaines, George Butler, and Arnold Schwarzenegger.

A rnold, back from projecting his Master Plan into the twenty-first century, has stopped rubbing his eyes. They are wide open, peering across his desk as I suggest an alternative way for him to consider this book.

"Well, why don't you think of this as just a book that covers ten years of real friendship. My life and your life when I was around with my camera and later with my camera crew making this Master Plan possible. You know, the years when we were having fun together."

"GEORRRGE," he says, reverting to a strong Austrian accent. "These pictures are not really me."

"But they are, Arnold. And they're me as well. Both of us did them," I say forcefully. "Put yourself in my position. I have a lot of time and good work in your career. Traveling around the world. Banging down the brick walls you faced. Would you deny me those ten years when I do my memoirs? I mean, this is my autobiography as well as yours."

Arnold reaches for an inlaid humidor. He takes out two Churchill-size cigars. He hands one to me, ignoring the question.

"No, thank you," I say. He knows perfectly well I don't smoke.

"It's very simple, my objection. The real one." He lights up. "This collection is incomplete."

I am surprised to see his hands are still shaking. This time he sees me notice them. I know he will make a mighty effort to bring them under control—just as he plans to bring my pictures under his control.

As he puffs his cigar, he succeeds—at least with his own hands. The pictures, I know then and there, will be public record. Social anthropology of America. A contemporary metaphor of our time: pain, beauty and power. Not under his absolute control.

But he has more to say, and as I always have with Arnold, I listen patiently.

"The reason this collection is incomplete," he says, gesturing with his Goliath of a cigar, "is because there are no pictures of me on the set of *The Villain,* my movie with Kirk Douglas in 1979. There are no pictures of me in *Stay Hungry.*"

"True."

"There are none of *Conan the Barbarian* in 1980," he adds quickly.

I start to protest.

"Hold on." He draws on his cigar. "Let me continue. There are no pictures of me in Hyannisport with the Kennedys. Nor me with Jerry Ford. Or Jimmy Carter. And not one of me in the White House. If you were doing your job, George . . ." He sweeps his cigar around his head at a picture on the wall of Ronald Reagan and the subject of this book. Glossy prints, all in color, of everyone he has just mentioned hang to the left and right, above and below. And there are *many* more of other grinning celebrities. "You should have made sure," Arnold continues, "to include them in this collection. This is my life. This is the way I see myself. This is ARNOLD."

"But Oak, my pictures are about light and form and character. I'm not interested in celebrities. I'm from New Hampshire, where the only celebrity is J. D. Salinger."

"Who?"

"A writer."

"I thought so."

"I am interested in you at your best. What you can really do. I care about your character and what you did with your body and how talented you really are. You can be like Fred Astaire or Baryshnikov. Really famous forever."

"No," he says resolutely.

"Yes," I reply with the conviction of someone who never gives up.

"Listen to me, George. I appreciate your interest in being a photographer. But all these pictures," he gestures at my boxes with an open hand, "are the past. They have no meaning. I try to put body-building behind me. We have to look forward now and do new things. BIGGER THINGS . . ."

"Oak . . ." I say, protesting, "you can't rewrite history."

He puffs his cigar and takes it from his mouth. His hands are absolutely steady and his body rigid.

"I have to go now," he replies. "Maria is waiting. I know you put a lot of work into these pictures. I think of that. But they are not right for me." He stretches lazily, controlling even his stiffness, breaking into his most charming smile.

"How is that Vietnam movie coming along?" he asks, referring to a project I have been working on for several years. It deals with the true story of a Green Beret medic who was blown away by the war and cured himself later through his encounters with wild grizzlies in the mountains of Montana.

"The script is almost finished," I say.

"Well, when it's done and you are ready to direct it, call me. I get you a studio deal. I know a lot of people at Universal. I tell them to do it for you. And they do it. *Twins* made 111 million dollars for Universal. They listen carefully to what I say these days. You tell me. I call them. If it's a big action picture with bears eating everything in sight, they do it."

Arnold stares at me in a thoughtful but extremely piercing way. There is a lot going on in his head behind those eyes. It is a moment of ambivalence about how he leads his life and what he knows I want to do with mine. We have done so much together and done it so well. But that is in the past and we are men of very different sensibilities, held together only by this ten years of old experience that Arnold at this moment really wants to forget. It is not Hollywood to honor friendship forever . . .

"But there cannot be any monkey business, George. It must be an action picture. None of this art bullshit."

I opened the palms of my hands toward him. "Wouldn't you ever like, in *Time* or *Newsweek,* to get a good review of your acting— or even with this book? I believe it'll get good reviews. Maybe the New York press will cover the opening of the show and write well of it."

"Fuck them."

I shake my head slowly and smile my most agreeable smile. It is exactly what Arnold knows I will do.

"Butler," my old friend says, "you never have enough money for a taxi, but . . ." He pauses and puffs his cigar. Then he clenches it in the side of his mouth and speaks through his teeth. "You are very smart. It's time for the BIG TIME. Don't waste yourself on these photographs. And remember . . ."

He stands up behind his desk and stretches again. Then he gives me the most piercing look of the afternoon.

"I always help you," he says, smiling.

George Butler
Holderness, N.H.

ACKNOWLEDGMENTS

I wish to express my gratitude to the following, without whose goodwill in the years of *Pumping Iron*, the books and movies we have made together would not have been possible: A. J. Adams, Jr., Elizabeth Alexander, Amelie Allen, Phillip Armour, Robert Asahina, Linda and Sam Baker, Igor Bakht, John Balik, Chip Barnes, Paul Barnes, Victor Barton, Jeff Bartz, Peter Beard, Bill Benenson, Belinda Breese, Burt Britton, Leon Brown, Cynthia Buchanan, Albert Busek, Richard Butler, Sean Callahan, Cornell Capa, Gaston Caperton, Michael Carlisle, Bob Cavallo, Marion Oates Charles, Earl Chase, Lawrence Chong, Joan Churchill, Susan Crutcher, Elissa Cullman, Peter Davis, Karen and Wayne DeMilia, Ira Deutchman, Robert Devereux, Ann Doherty, Michael P. Dominick, William Ducas.

Carla Dunlap, Larry Fabian, Louis Ferrigno, Robert Fiore, Bev Francis, David Gamble, Jerome Gary, Tracy Gary, Veronica Geng, Joe Gold, Vicki Goldberg, Dan and Jane Green, Jon Gruber, Brooke Hayward, Bernard Heng, John Herman, Rupert Hitzig, Aude Holden-Hindley, Tom Hurwitz, Annette Insdorf, Nick Irens, Laurie Jewell, Anne C. Johnson, Elizabeth Johnson, Laurie Jones, Ed Jubinville, Pierre Kalfon, John Karol, Mike Katz, Tom Kinney, Mike Kissel, Seymour Klein, Zabo Koszewski, Jane Kurson, Annie Leibovitz, Leo Lerman.

Edward Lider, Belinda Loh, Jim Macida, John Mack, Wendy MacKenzie, Peter Magowan, Paul Marbury, Pat McBaine, C. C. McGettigan, Jr., Ian McLaughlin, Rachel McLish, Teri McLuhan, Angela Miller, Pat Mitchel, Wendy Moonan, Ann Morton, Marty Moskof, Serge Nubret, Jeff Norman, Leonard R. Olsen, Jr., B. S. Ong, Abe Peck, Stella and Bill Pence, Mark and Linda Peroff, Virginia Perry, Pickle Pine Associates, George Plimpton, Philip Pillsbury, Lynn Povitch, Renée Rabb, Tobie Rafelson, Delfina Rattazzi, Fabienne Rawley, Peter and Sandy Riva, Robbie Robinson, Jonathan Rodgers, Morley Safer, DeWitt Sage, Jr., Richard Schickel, Stephen Schiff, Jeremy and Wendy Schmidt, Peter Schmidt, Maria Shriver, Larry Silk, Jack Skow, Liz Smith, George Snyder, Philip Sorace.

Joe Spieler, Charles Stainbach, Rufus Standefer, Stephan Starr, Nick and Lydia Staskiewicz, Gloria Steinem, Suzanne St. Pierre, Mark Strand, Robert Straus, Howard Stringer, David and Barbara Stone, Dyanna Taylor, Mary Taylor, Tom Thayer, Al Thomas, David Thompson, Rusty Unger, Tony Unger, Thomas Vaughan, Oliver Vaughan, Susan Victor, Kimon Voyages, Sam Wagstaff, William Walton, Rickie Wayne, Ben Weider, Joe Weider, Richard S. West, Clark Whelton, Sir Gordon White, Jack Wiener, Bruce Williamson, Tom Wolfe, William Woodward, III, Chris Wright, Jamie Wyeth, J. David Wyles, Lloyd Young, Frank and Christine Zane, Bobby Zarem, Lucinda Ziesing.

PHOTOGRAPHER'S NOTE

All the photographs in this book were taken with a Leica M4 camera and a Leitz Summilux f/1.4 35mm lens. Throughout I used Kodak Tri-X film with available light only.